SAIL YOUR CANOE

John Bull

How To Add Sails To Your Canoe

© John Bull 1989

British Library Cataloguing in Publication Data

Bull, John
    Sail your canoe.
    1. Canoes. Cruising – Manuals
    I. Title
    797.1 ' 22

    ISBN 0 904405 94 X

Text processing by: Reachword Limited, Sudbrooke Lincoln, LN2 2QU
Printed by Hi-Tec Print, Dinnington, S. Yorks, S31 YJJ

This book is available from all specialist canoe shops, and booksellers. It can be obtained direct from the publishers, together with most other books for canoeists and mountain sports. Send for a copy of our catalogue.

CORDEE
3a De Montfort Street, Leicester Great Britain, LE1 7HD

John MacGregor. M.A. The founder of canoeing as a sport 1865.

CONTENTS

IT HAS ALL BEEN DONE BEFORE

The sport of canoeing was thrust into prominence by the adventures of John MacGregor in his canoe Rob Roy in which he toured European rivers in the summer of 1865. Subsequently he wrote an account of his travels, 'A Thousand Miles in Rob Roy' and it was this book that aroused the interest of the young men of Victorian England and the United States and led to the development of the sailing canoe.

In these early days most of the canoes were of the Rob Roy type, about fifteen or so feet in length with a thirty inch beam and usually clinker built to a very high standard. She had a small standing lugsail and a fore sail although she had no rudder nor any means of preventing leeway and could only run before the wind.

The Rob Roy design was quickly obsolete. The canoes soon became much more sophisticated, sail areas were increased, ballast was added and rudders and some sort of keel became the norm. The first of the Baden-Powell Nautilus designs appeared, sailing canoes were rapidly becoming miniature yachts and a division between the racing fraternity and the cruising men was soon apparent. There were many fine travelling boats built at the end of the last century and some prodigious journeys made. After MacGregor's exploits in the sixties in which he made extensive cruises in the Baltic and the Middle East there were men like Roger Anderson, who was later to become a trustee of the British Maritime Museum at Greenwich, who in company with a rather strange Swedish sailor, Herman Lantz, sailed in two canoes from Stockholm to St. Petersburgh, now Leningrad. The journey of four hundred and twenty-four miles took them twenty-six days, an average of sixteen and a half miles a day. The best day's run was of thirty-four miles while there were many days they managed to make thirty miles. Of course there were days lost while they waited for the weather on the more exposed passages, the longest of these being some sixteen miles from Sodarm to Lagskar in the Swedish Archipelago.

Warrington Baden-Powell, the brother of the founder of the Boy Scout movement Robert Baden-Powell also made extensive cruises in Sweden in the third of his Nautilus boats at about the same period. He was well known as a sailing canoe designer and was the first challenger for the International Challenge Cup put up by the New York Canoe Club.

In America sailing canoes had quickly developed from the first English designs that they had acquired in 1870, in general the American boats were lighter, relying on the live weight of the crew rather than the lead ballast the English boats carried. In spite of the enthusiasm with which they developed their racing boats there were many great voyagers among them.

In 1874 Nathaniel Bishop had sailed and paddled his canoe, the Maria Theresa, an early Nautilus design of W. Baden-Powell's but built of overlapping sheets of paper built up in layers rather as we build G.R.P. boats today, from Quebec to Florida, a staggering distance of some two thousand five hundred miles.

Charles Neide, who was secretary of the American Canoe Association in 1882, started from the Lake George meet in the north of New York State and made a journey of two thousand five hundred miles through rivers, lakes and inland waterways to Pensacola in Florida. Some trip!

Another formidable canoeist of the period was the American Frederick A. Fenger. He was a professional naval architect who had designed many yachts and was a very experienced canoe and small boat sailor. What he is remembered for today is his remarkable sailing canoe, Yakaboo. Yakaboo, which means goodbye in one of the West Indian dialects, was a powerful seaboat, seventeen feet overall and thirty-nine inches on the beam and was rigged as a ketch with the then fashionable batwing sails of some ninety square feet. Yakaboo had several unique features, she used oars instead of a paddle, and did not have a rudder but was steered by sliding the centreboard fore and aft.

In 1911 Fenger sailed from Grenada, in the West Indies, through the chain of islands that constitute the Windward and Leeward Islands to the Island of Saba at the far northern end of the archipelago. Many of the passages he made were fifty or sixty miles long and exposed to the full force of the wind and sea, fifteen hundred miles of it to port and starboard, only the narrow island chain offering any sort of shelter. That Yakaboo completed her voyage successfully says much for her master, designer and builder.

The ultimate and almost inevitable challenge was to be the crossing of the Atlantic. This was first taken up by Captain Franz Romer in 1928 who sailed and paddled his way from Portugal, via the Canary Islands to St. Thomas in the Virgin Islands. The crossing from the Canaries to the West Indies had taken him eight weeks and the exhausted Captain was found asleep in his canoe in St. Thomas's harbour after having covered over four thousand miles, through many gales and even two hurricanes.

This Herculean task was again taken up by another German, Hannes Lindeman, who after several attempts was finally successful in 1955. Following much the same course as Romer he crossed in sixty-five days, in a twenty-three foot by thirty inch dugout canoe called Liberia. She had a two hundred and fifty pound lead keel and was rigged in an old fashioned way with a gaff main sail and a square sail set on the same mast.

Before Lindeman had even returned to his native Hamburg he was planning a second attempt, this time in a folding canoe, a Klepper, the Liberia 3. She was modified for the voyage though to no great extent. The mainmast was fitted with back stays and the deck reinforced with extra canvas. Again she was rigged with a gaff mainsail and a square sail on the mainmast but also carried a mizzen sail and an outrigger made from half a car inner tube which he lashed to a paddle and carried to leeward. In spite of this Lindeman was capsized twice towards the end of his voyage and arrived in St. Martin after seventy-six days at sea.

There is no doubt that sailing canoes do have considerable potential as cruising boats, though perhaps not to the extremes chosen by Romer and Lindeman. They make able beach cruisers even to the extent of providing rather Spartan accommodation for their crew. The canoe world has largely been taken over by the more commonly seen competition boats, indeed many people find it hard to believe that canoes can be driven by sails without upsetting and without the need for daring do.

THE REALITY

People are often surprised to learn that canoes make good sailing craft, the conventional wisdom is that they don't. However, properly set up they are capable of going well to windward and will come about as smartly as many another craft. Even a long flat bottomed cruising canoe will need no more than the odd paddle stroke to get her through the wind, a situation that our forefathers were more than familiar with in their days of sail.

Almost any canoe can carry some sort of sail to its advantage, it will greatly extend the range of the boat and will be less demanding on the crew, one can sail for far longer than you can paddle, particularly in difficult conditions. Sail in combination with paddles is a very efficient means of travelling.

Of course travelling canoes should not be compared with dinghys for performance, the canoe will usually have more pounds per square foot of sail than the dinghy, it's a question of horses for courses. If you really want to go fast then the ten square metre sailing canoe is among the fastest boats in the world but you wouldn't want to go far on it.

The range of canoe hulls to which sails can be fitted is so wide that it is probably better to explain the design principles involved, they are not difficult to understand or apply, rather than to give specific instructions for one type of canoe. This approach will also allow you to try out different rigs on your boat, in itself a pleasant and fascinating occupation.

The pleasure to be had from sailing a canoe is out of all proportion to the very modest investment it requires. I hope you will get as much enjoyment from sailing your canoe as I have from mine.

HOW MUCH SAIL?

The first question we need to answer is how big a sail do you need?

If you only want to use the sail purely as an 'auxiliary', to run before the wind when the opportunity presents itself, then eight or ten square feet of sail will be plenty. This will be enough to push the hull along at its maximum, probably about four knots. For downwind sailing only the rig can be kept very simple, a small sail with a short mast and spar that is convenient to use and easy to stow away when not required. You will not need leeboards or a rudder, course corrections can be made with the sail or a paddle. This is very much the sort of rig that could be of great benefit to a sea canoeist.

The most important aspect of the relationship between the hull and the rig is that of the total weight of the craft and its crew to the sail area. For a seagoing canoe this could be in the order of between five or six pounds per square foot of sail area. For an inland flat water craft perhaps between four and five pounds per square foot depending on its purpose. An International Ten Square Metre Sailing Canoe has about three point five pounds per square foot but these really are the formula one machines of sailing canoes and are very demanding to sail.

If you have more ambitious sailing plans then you're going to need a more sophisticated and powerful rig that will drive the boat to windward. It will also have to be equipped with leeboards or a dagger board, to resist the sideways drift induced by the sail and a rudder for steering.

For a single seat touring hull between twenty-five and thirty square feet of sail is about right and for a two seater forty-five to fifty-five square feet should suffice. Some of the heavier touring boats with a beam of thirty or more inches can carry sixty or seventy square feet to advantage, particularly those with a flatish bottom like many of the Canadian canoes.

Don't be tempted to overcanvas the boat, seagoing canoes in particular are best sailed from within their cockpits, you need a working rig that is comfortable to sail with not something that is a taskmaster. In very light weather it is better to set extra sails, tops'ls, stays'ls or watersails and the like. I also prefer to set a separate storm sail of about forty per cent of the working sail rather than reef the main. I have yet to find a really good reefing system that suits canoes.

ALL YOU NEED TO KNOW

When a boat sails downwind it is literally just blown along, but a boat sailing across the wind or at an angle into the wind converts the airflow over its sails partly into forward drive and partly into a sideways drift.

There are two principal components, wind and water, and it is their relationship to one another that we need to understand. We need to be able to identify the points on which the forces of wind and water act.

1) THE CENTRE OF EFFORT (CE) developed by a sail or combination of sails is that point, theoretically at any rate, at which we can say that all the forces generated by the sail act. In practice we can find the CE simply by cutting the sail shape out of thick cartridge paper and finding its point of balance. Use a convenient scale, say $1\frac{1}{2}$ inches to the foot then $\frac{1}{8}$ represents 1 inch which is quite accurate enough.

The CE for a triangular sail may be found by dividing a side and drawing a line to the opposite corner, where the lines intersect is the CE. It is also the point at which the shape will balance. For multi sails rigs the CE will lie on the line connecting the individual CE's.

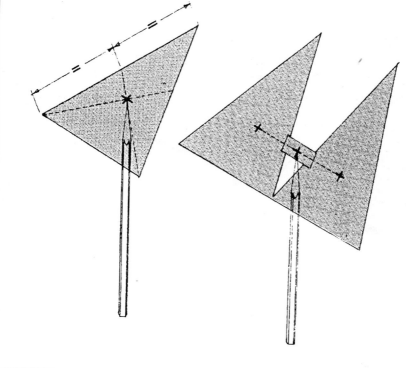

If you try this out on a few different sail shapes you will soon see that the tall narrow shapes, such as most modern racing boats have, have a relatively high CE. Canoes, because of their narrow beam and lack of bearing are more suited to sails that have a low CE. The lower the CE is to the hull the less the overturning force will be. Some of the more old fashioned rigs that had a long low profile are of more value to canoes.

2) THE CENTRE OF LATERAL RESISTANCE, (CLR). This is another very useful theoretical point at which we can assume that all the resistance to the sideways drift of the boat acts.

As with the CE of the sail we can cut out the underwater shape of the hull and its leeboard or daggerboard from stiff paper or card. All we need to know is the line of the lateral resistance, at this stage we can ignore the rudder.

It is the underwater shape ONLY that is needed. If the board is cut out separately and tacked on with a tiny piece of sticky tape it can be moved around more easily.

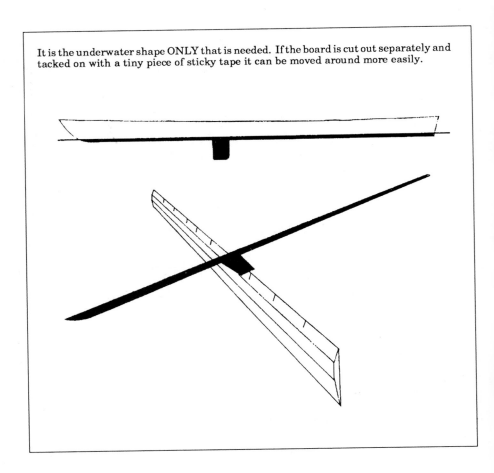

If the sails and the hull are to be in the right relationship to one another then the CE of the sails must be in line with the line of the CLR of the hull.

Canoe hulls have very little lateral resistance because of their shallow draught, they depend almost entirely on the leeboard or daggerboard. The CLR can be moved significantly by increasing the size of the board, which moves the CLR foreward or by increasing the size of the rudder which will move it aft. A little juggling with the rake of the mast and the relative sizes of the board and the rudder will usually solve most balance problems. You may find with some arrangements that the line of lateral resistance does not pass through the board, this does not matter, it is much more important that you line up the CE and CLR.

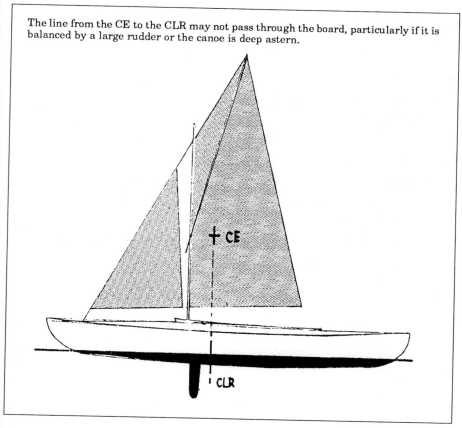

The line from the CE to the CLR may not pass through the board, particularly if it is balanced by a large rudder or the canoe is deep astern.

The state of balance you are aiming for is that the boat should turn slowly into the wind when you let go the steering. This is called weather helm, the opposite, with the boat turning away from the wind is called lee helm. Minor adjustments can be made to the balance by altering the fore and aft trim of the boat or by altering the set of the sail where possible. It all sounds very much more complicated than it really is, so don't be put off, just tackle one job at a time.

THE PRACTICAL SOLUTION

The mast position on most conversions is usually determined by its having to go at the front of the cockpit and unless you're sure that you want to start cutting holes in the deck this is the only possible site. Actually, making a hole in the deck is not so serious, there are plenty of rubber or plastic blanks available these days from D.I.Y. shops or electrical suppliers. On two seaters it's sometimes worth considering stepping the mast at the after end of the front cockpit.

Start by cutting out the shape of the sail you're going to use from stiff paper at $1^1/_2$ inches to the foot. Find its point of balance, the CE. Then measure how far behind the mast the CE is and transfer this measurement at full size to your canoe. This will be the position of the board.

The size of the sail determines how big the board will need to be, about 3% of the sail area is usually sufficient. The table below gives the sizes of the board for different sail areas, remember that this is the size BELOW the waterline.

Sail area	Board depth (ins)			
square feet	at 6" wide	at 9" wide	at 12" wide	at 15" wide
15	11.25			
20	15.00			
25	18.75			
30	22.50			
35		17.50		
40		20.00		
45		22.50		
50			18.75	
55			20.60	
60			22.50	
65				19.5
70				21.0

The rudder is also an important item, not only for its steering facility but also for its contribution to the lateral plane. Generally the rudder should be about half the size of the board and this can be simply deduced from the table for the board size.

In practice the CE is not directly above the CLR as we have so far assumed but should be 5 or 6% of the waterline length ahead of it. It is a happy coincidence that when the rudder is included in the calculation it moves the CLR aft by about the right amount.

That's about all there is to the basic theory, you don't need to worry too much about absolute accuracy, the theory is to some extent arbitrary. When the wind fills the sails and the boat heels then the geometry alters considerably but these simple methods will get you close to the correct answer more quickly than just guessing. You will have done well if it all works out perfectly the first time, there's usually a bit of fiddling needed to get the boat to perform at her best.

If you have not sailed a canoe before, then choose a quiet day for your first trip, you need to be able to give your attention to the boat rather than having to concentrate on survival. This is the time to check that the balance of the rig and the hull is O.K. See how altering the fore and aft trim of the boat affects her. You can reduce the size of the board relative to the rudder by raising it slightly. Don't make more than one adjustment at a time or you'll get confused as to what is affecting what.

SAILING RIGS

Just about every kind of sailing rig has been tried on canoes at one time or another and most work more or less, so it really is a matter of personal choice as to which is best for you. Technically it is more efficient to use one larger sail rather than a number of small sails but the loss of efficiency for a cruising boat is often more than compensated for by gains in other directions. You are relatively immobile in a canoe so the ease of handling the rig at sea is important and it is usually easier to set or douse a sail completely than to be messing about with reefs. The shape of the sail often suffers rather badly when it is reefed so multi sailed rigs are worth considering.

Sails on a seagoing canoe should always be able to weathercock freely so that in an emergency the sheet can be let go and the boat relieved of the pressure. The small masts should be freestanding so there is nothing to obstruct the sail from weathercocking and of course sheets should never be made fast but always kept in the hand.

The lateen sail is a fine rig for small craft and particularly for sailing canoes, it deserves to be better known and more widely used than it is. It is basically an equilateral triangle and has a very low centre of effort set on a short mast, if the leading edge is sleeved to the spar it can develop quite high efficiencies, that is more drive for the least overturning force of almost all the rigs.

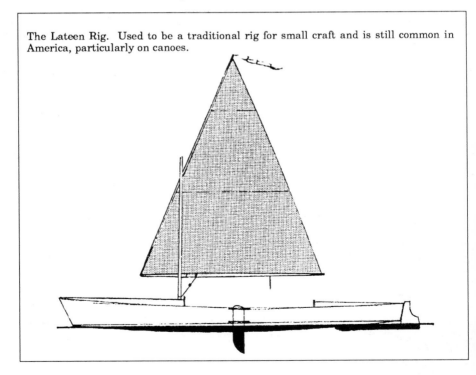

The Lateen Rig. Used to be a traditional rig for small craft and is still common in America, particularly on canoes.

14

The description to be given here of the construction of a lateen sail may be applied to almost any sail. To make this thirty square foot sail you will need 6 metres of 30 inch wide $1\frac{1}{2}$ oz spinnaker cloth. Lay it out and join the pieces with double sided sticky tape as shown.

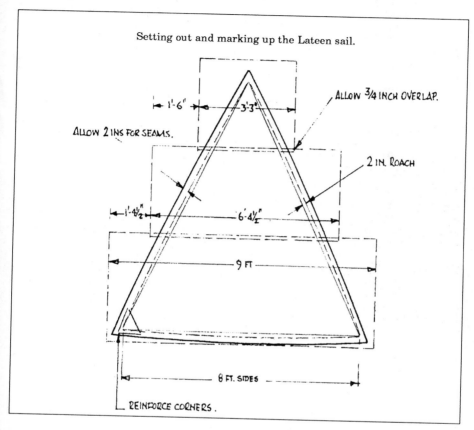

Setting out and marking up the Lateen sail.

ALLOW ¾ INCH OVERLAP.

ALLOW 2 INS FOR SEAMS.

1'-6"

3'-3"

2 IN. ROACH

1'-4½"

6'-4½"

9 FT

8 FT. SIDES

REINFORCE CORNERS.

Mark out with chalk and a long springy batten held down with a few building bricks. The edges of the sail are long curves called the roach, about 2 inches of roach for this length of side is about right and it will help the sail to take up a better shape when it is set. Do remember to add on a couple of inches to the overall dimensions to allow for seaming. When the sail is cut to shape fit a small triangle of cloth of approximately 9 inches into each corner of the sail as reinforcement. The edge seams can now be folded over and secured with double sided sticky tape to make a 1 inch seam all round the sail. All the seams can now be sewn on an ordinary domestic sewing machine using polyester thread, each seam should be double sewn.

On a lateen sail only the leading edge is fastened to the spar, you will need to fit six or seven $\frac{1}{4}$ inch brass eyelets along one edge and a further one in the remaining corner.

When the sail is rigged to the spars the leading edge should not be over tensioned or you will get a nasty ruckle in the leading edge of the sail. The third corner of the sail, the clew, is secured by the outhaul to the after end of the boom. By adjusting the tension of the outhaul we can alter the shape of the sail. It needs to be slacker in calm weather so that the sail can take up a full shape and to be tightened as the wind strengthens to give a flatter shape.

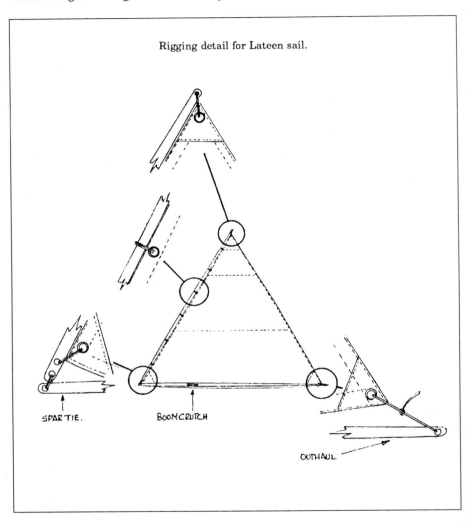

Rigging detail for Lateen sail.

SPAR TIE.

BOOM CRUTCH

OUTHAUL

The mast and spars can be made from any good quality straight grained wood, spruce is the traditional material but I have always used columbian pine, it's a little heavier but you can cut a thinner spar. Make them to the dimensions given in the drawing.

Mast and spar detail. All holes shown are $^3/_8$" diameter. Finish with several coats of raw linseed oil and paint the last three or four inches of the spars with white paint, mostly for protection but it looks nice too.

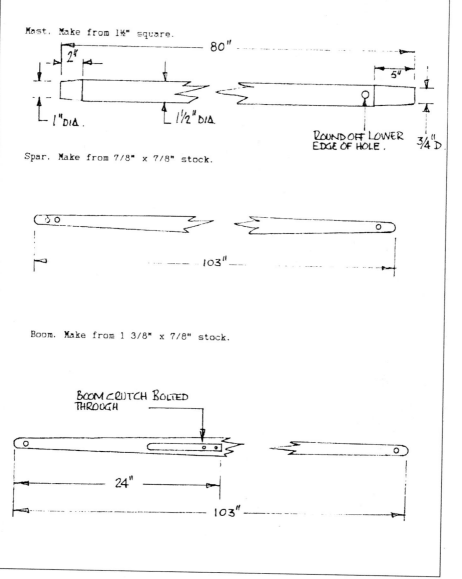

Mast. Make from 1½" square.

Spar. Make from 7/8" x 7/8" stock.

Boom. Make from 1 3/8" x 7/8" stock.

There is no reason why you should not use aluminium tube or bamboo cane if you can get it, both are excellent for spar making.

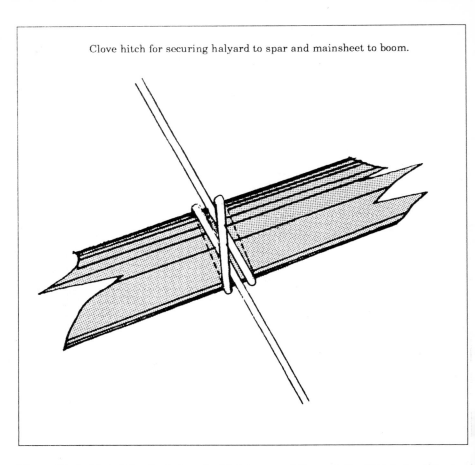

Clove hitch for securing halyard to spar and mainsheet to boom.

The sail is held aloft by the halyard which is passed through the $3/_8$th hole at the top of the mast, smooth off the lower corners of this hole. The halyard is secured to the spar by a clove hitch and at its other end to a small cleat screwed to the mast.

Cleat, screwed to mast as shown, to secure the halyard.

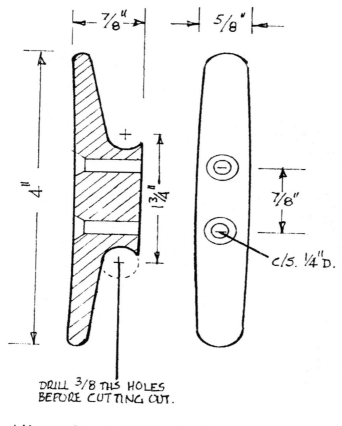

DRILL 3/8 THIS HOLES
BEFORE CUTTING OUT.

MAKE FROM HARDWOOD
MAHOGANY LOOKS NICE.

Make sure that you make the halyard long enough to lower the sail and stow it below decks if that's your intention.

The boom is secured to the mast by a boom crutch and is kept in position by the kicking strap. Sailing canoes almost always need a boom, they are too narrow to provide the proper sheeting angle for the sail without.

Boom crutch detail. Make from 1¼" hardwood. Through bolt to boom with ¼" bolts.

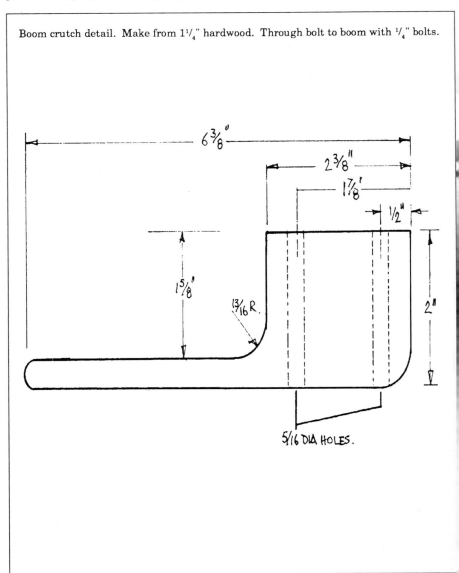

The boom crutch can be made from 1¼ inch hardwood. The dimensions are not critical but its fitting to the boom is. It is best through bolted to the boom.

Kicking strap detail. Make from $1/8$" or $3/16$" diameter nylon line, the wooden button is to allow the sail to be detached from the mast for stowing. Under normal conditions the kicking strap is kept tight, to hold the boom crutch into the mast and to prevent the boom from lifting.

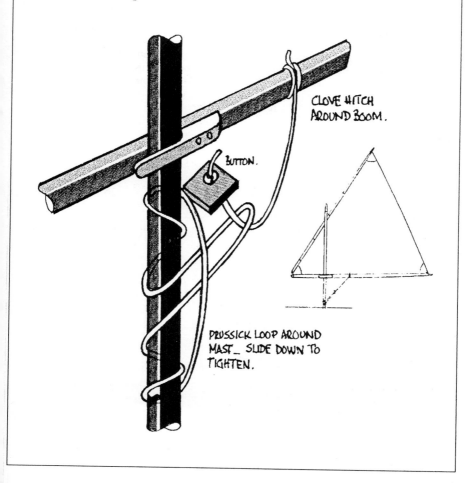

CLOVE HITCH AROUND BOOM.

BUTTON.

PRUSSICK LOOP AROUND MAST_ SLIDE DOWN TO TIGHTEN.

The kicking strap is in two parts to facilitate the removal of the sail from the mast. The single part, with the wooden button on, is secured to the boom by a clove hitch. The lower part is a prussick loop which has the useful attribute in that when it is slack it can be easily slid up and down the mast but when it is pulled tight it will lock into position and stay put.

When the sail is rigged on the boat the halyard is normally attached to the spar at a third of the way up. A certain amount of adjustment to the CE of the sail in relation to the CLR and the boat's balance can be made by varying this position.

The mainsheet can be fastened to the boom by a clove hitch and positioned so that it falls conveniently to hand. Make it up from fairly large diameter rope, around half an inch or so. This is not for strength but because smaller rope, which is quite strong enough, is often uncomfortable in the hand, particularly when your hands are wet and cold. Make sure too that the mainsheet is long enough to allow the sail to rotate through 180 degrees so that you have enough rope to allow the sail to weathercock fully.

There are several different ways by which the mast may be fitted to the hull. It is supported at two points, at deck level and at the foot, the mast step. Through the deck is neatest but other than that the choice is to suit your canoe.

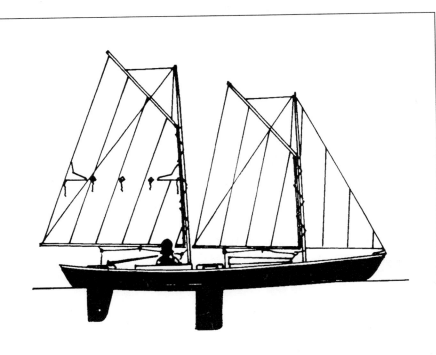

This is Phil Bolger's 20 ft O.A. Schooner rigged sailing canoe, probably the only ballasted canoe in use today, she has one hundred pounds of lead at the bottom of her four foot dagger board and sets 125 sq. ft. of sail. The stripped hull weighs about 150 lbs. The fore hatch can be raised to give camping accommodation for two.

Different methods of fitting the mast to the hull, each of these methods can be applied to the thwart of an open canoe.

1. Through a hole, in the deck or thwart.

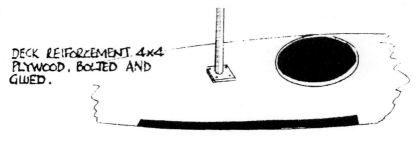

DECK REIFORCEMENT 4×4 PLYWOOD. BOLTED AND GLUED.

2. Brass or S.S. gate bolted to inside of cockpit or screwed to thwart.

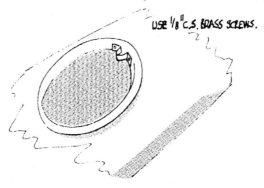

USE ⅛" C.S. BRASS SCREWS.

3. Plywood gate bolted to underside of deck or thwart.

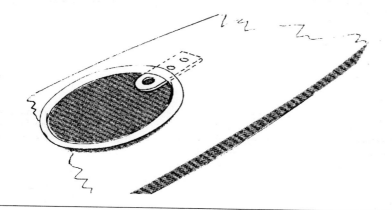

The mast step can be made up as shown from hardwood. It allows some adjustment of the rake of the mast and hence the position of the CE in relation to the CLR. The lower platform of the step can be fastened to the bottom of the canoe simply by sticking it with araldite or epoxy resin. I usually bolt mine through from underneath.

Mast step. Make from $2^1/_2$" x $1^1/_4$" hardwood stock.

The lower platform is bolted through the bottom of the hull, the upper block is screwed onto the lower and can be adjusted fore and aft to alter the rake of the mast.

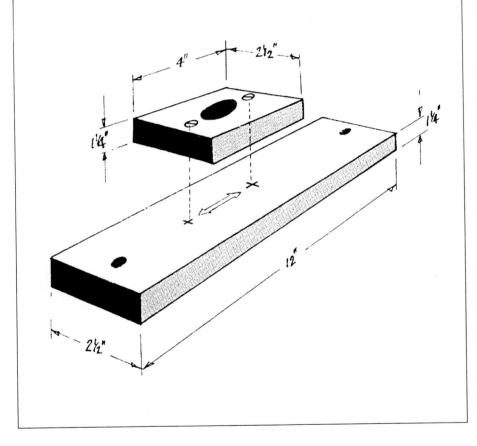

Of course there are many other sails and rigs that are suitable for canoes, some were expressly designed for sailing canoes about a hundred years ago during the golden years of canoe sailing. The Cincinnati Lateen is one such. Very similar to the ordinary lateen sail but it uses an even shorter mast and the spar is set up at a much steeper angle. It is likely to have a higher efficiency to windward. Construction is much the same as for the lateen described at the beginning of this section.

The Cincinnati Lateen rig. Good windward efficiency although the very long spar can be a problem. When the sail is down the very short mast presents little wind resistance.

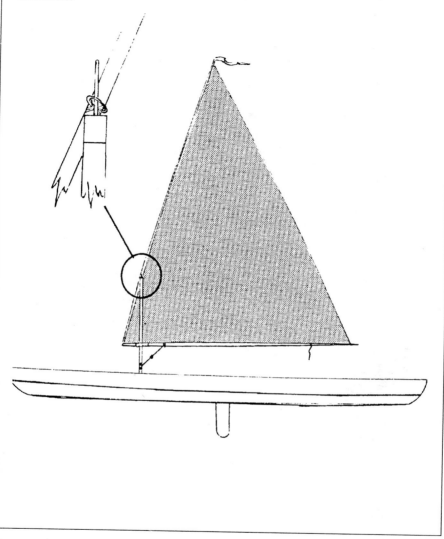

The standing lugsail was also a sail that was much used in the old days, even on international racing canoes of the 1880's. It's a good sail for canoes, simple in construction and satisfactory in use. It is essentially a lateen sail with the part ahead of the mast cut off. A boom crutch is not needed as the kicking strap is repositioned at the foreward end of the boom and serves both purposes.

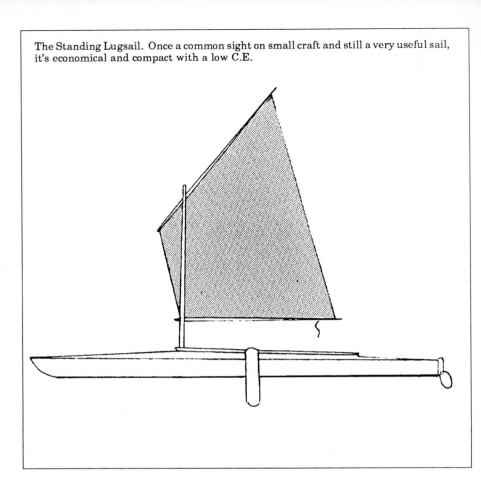

The Standing Lugsail. Once a common sight on small craft and still a very useful sail, it's economical and compact with a low C.E.

These sails are all well tried and tested but there is still plenty of opportunity for the experimeter today. The sails that are used on sailboards look as though they could be usefully adapted and there is news that the aerodynamicist Tony Marchaj of Southampton University has recently discovered that the Pacific Crab Claw sails are more efficient than jib headed sails apart from the last few degrees to windward.

A Fijian sea-going canoe. Modern research has shown the sail, made from pandanus matting to be outstandingly effective and in the hands of a skilled crew capable of very high speeds. Simple or crude?

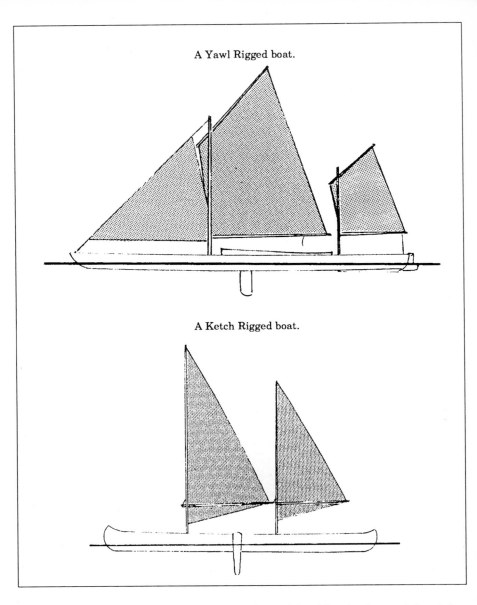

A Yawl Rigged boat.

A Ketch Rigged boat.

There are similar opportunities with rigs. Many of the old racing boats and cruising canoes were ketch rigged. (The terminology in this paper uses yawl to denote a rig where the mizzen sail is essentially a balancing sail and does not contribute in any significant way to the drive. With a ketch rigged boat the mizzen plays a considerable part in driving the boat. It's worth making clear what is intended by these terms because there is often considerable confusion and argument over them).

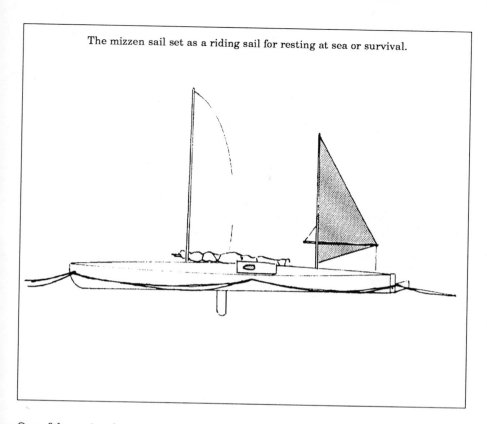

The mizzen sail set as a riding sail for resting at sea or survival.

One of the main advantages in using several sails is that it allows the rig to be spread out in a horizontal line rather than allowing the CE to climb upwards as the rig is increased. Such rigs also have the inherent ability to balance the boat on different points of sailing and in different weather and sea conditions, even to the extent that in extremis the main on a yawl can be stowed, the mizzen sheeted in hard and the boat allowed to weathercock into the weather. At this stage the crew should retire below and pray.

Whichever design path you choose to follow there are one or two useful maxims that probably apply to all of them. Firstly, beware of over complication, it may work fine in your garden at home but it's not the same at sea. The KISS principle, Keep It Simple Stupid, applies very much to sailing canoes. Simple things almost always work. Similarly, don't be tempted to splatter blocks and stainless steel goodies all over the boat. Apart from the needless expense they are just not necessary to handle these little rigs. A hole through the mast is perfectly adequate as a halyard sheave, wooden buttons substitute without fault for snap shackles or karabiners. One of the great virtues of this kind of approach is that when things break or wear out they are simply and cheaply replaced, even if it happens at sea. Don't forget to leave your sails with the freedom to weathercock and make sure that you can perform all the sail handling operations from your seat.

LEEBOARDS, DAGGERS AND RUDDERS.

Leeboards are 'old fashioned'. Well yes they are but they are still a remarkably simple and effective way of projecting the lateral plane below the boat. They are rarely seen in this country but are quite common in the United States and still very much part of the design repertoire of American designers. One of their great assets, particularly for canoes, is that they don't clutter up an already restricted internal space.

There are many variations on the theme, no doubt you will be able to think of a few more. The conventional way of fitting leeboards to a canoe is by means of a rail clamped across the cockpit, the weakness tends often to be in the fitting of the screws into the ends of the rail. In my experience a far superior method are rope hangings, it looks crude although I would prefer to call it simple, and has never ever let me down. Surprisingly the rope hangings often last two or three seasons without much apparent wear. It is usually possible to secure the inboard end of the lanyard to a secure point, a deck plate internally or externally mounted, or on canvas covered canoes to the nearest frame. It is perfectly reasonable to use a single leeboard that has its lanyard secured in the centre of the boat. The only real drawback to this method is that the water is inclined to run down your arm as you change the board from side to side.

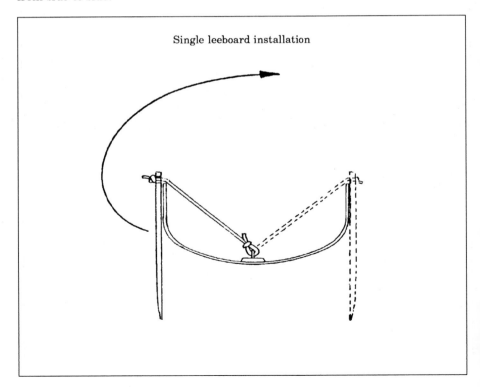

Single leeboard installation

30

Alternative methods of fitting leeboards.

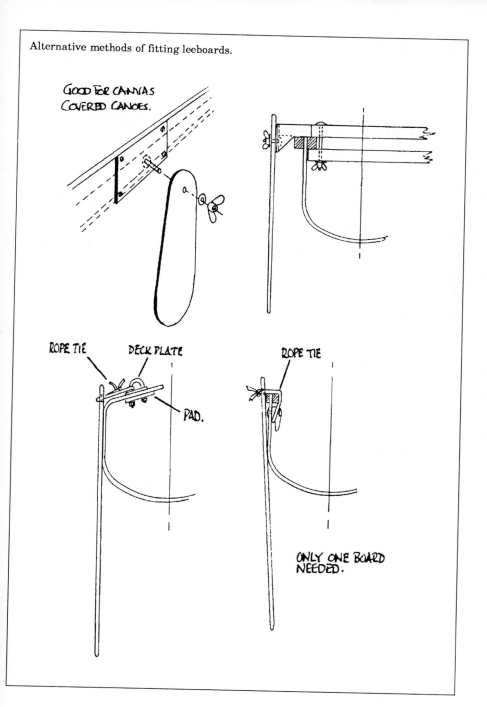

GOOD FOR CANVAS
COVERED CANOES.

ROPE TIE   DECK PLATE

PAD.

ROPE TIE

ONLY ONE BOARD
NEEDED.

When you make the board don't leave corners on the bottom, cut them to a nice radius so that the bottom is almost semicircular, sharp corners only create drag. Similarly the cross section of the board should be shaped to a streamlined shape to improve the water flow over it and reduce its drag.

Leeboard Detail. Make up from two pieces of $^3/_8$", 9mm plywood.
Sharp corners produce turbulence and drag.

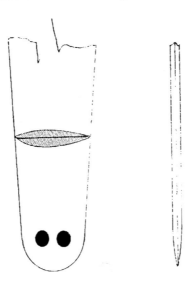

Leeboards are better with some ballast, cast lead as shown for about the right amount. Paint the area to be cast into with Waterglass, obtainable fom a good ironmongers, this will prevent the wood from burning.

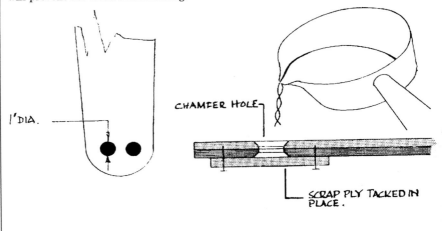

I'DIA.

CHAMFER HOLE

SCRAP PLY TACKED IN PLACE.

Another method that works very well is to mount the board as a daggerboard through a pair of hardwood cleats that are through bolted to the side of the boat. A six inch space between the cleats is quite enough to hold the board but of course you do have to have a boat with reasonably flat sides. You can compensate for some curvature by packing behind the cleats but there are limits to this. The daggerboard stays on the same side of the boat whichever tack you're on, if this does create any imbalance by being offset on one tack it is certainly not noticeable and it does mean you only have one board to bother with. This is a very simple and highly effective method and is to be recommended where possible over the others.

Daggerboard detail. Daggerboards are the same size as a leeboard but only one is needed. Ballast is not needed.

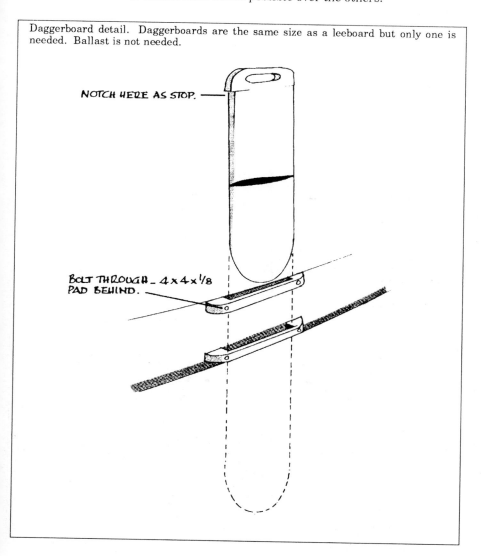

NOTCH HERE AS STOP.

BOLT THROUGH _ 4 x 4 x 1/8
PAD BEHIND.

Rudders can be rather trickier to fit, the main problem being getting a secure base for the hangings on the hull. You really do need to be able to reach into the end of the boat to through bolt the hanging. If the ends are closed by a bulkhead self tapping screws will hold well if the laminate is thick enough to take them, a good $^1/_8$ or $^3/_{16}$ths is needed. Use bedding compound between the two surfaces. Failing this you could try making the hanging rather larger in its contact area and araldite it to the hull. This is not as crude as it sounds, if you're careful and patient with the fitting of the two surfaces it will be a very tight bond. After all the decking in most modern aircraft is only glued together, epoxy bonding is immensely strong if it is done properly.

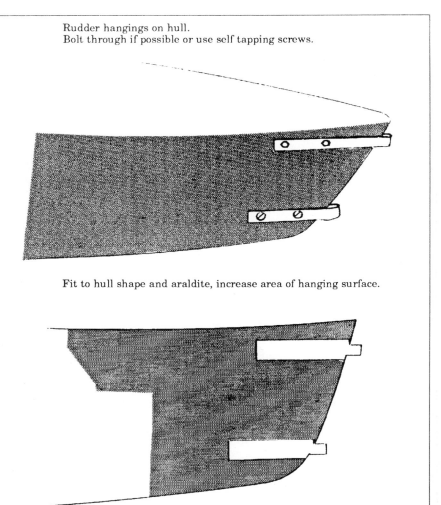

Rudder hangings on hull.
Bolt through if possible or use self tapping screws.

Fit to hull shape and araldite, increase area of hanging surface.

On canvas covered canoes the rudder hangings should be positioned over the gunwhale at the top and one of the lower stringers, use a bedding compound and something like $^3/_4$ inch No. 8 brass screws.

The design of the rudder itself is a subject about which whole books have been written, there are however principally two main types, shallow and horizontal rudders, low aspect ratio, and deep vertical rudders, high aspect ratio. The former are the simplest and the latter the most efficient.

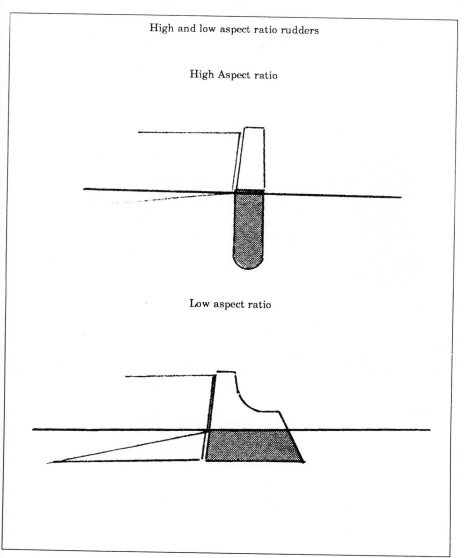

High and low aspect ratio rudders

High Aspect ratio

Low aspect ratio

Being a simple sort of soul I almost always choose the simplest solution, the low aspect ratio rudder. Its efficiency can be considerably enhanced if it is fitted with pressure fences made from 1 inch aluminium angle and although I have sailed in rough seas I have yet to find my rudder out of the water and inoperative, a charge that is often levelled at this type of rudder. As with the board the rudder should be shaped to present a streamline shape to the water. The metal fittings on both the rudder and the hull are usually made from $1/_{16}$th stainless steel or brass and should be through bolted wherever possible. Steering is by two lines that are lead to the cockpit and secured via lengths of shockcord to keep them under tension, this also has the advantage that when you are paddling the rudder automatically centres itself. You can either steer by hand or take the rudder lines via some kind of foot steering bar, it's a question of personal preference.

Low aspect ratio rudder, detail. Don"t forget that the designed area represents the area below the waterline. The pressure fence at the bottom of the rudder is important, it markedly increases the hydrodynamic efficiency of the blade.

Make from $3/_8$", 9mm plywood. All bolted assembly.

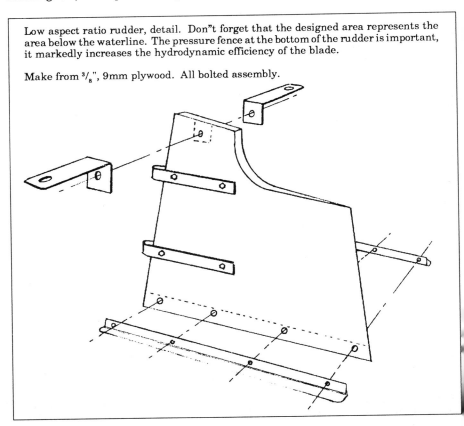

The high aspect ratio rudder is a little more complicated to make in order that the blade should be able to swing upwards as the boat enters shallow water. This can be achieved in several ways, by a ballasted or metal blade, by a length of shockcord or by a manual line. They all have their points and there is little to choose between them.

High aspect ratio rudder, detail. Make up rudder head as a sandwich of three $3/8$" plywood pieces, glue together. A metal blade of $1/8$" or $3/16$" aluminium may be substituted, reduce thickness of centre of sandwich appropriately. Don't forget that the designed area represents the area below the waterline only.

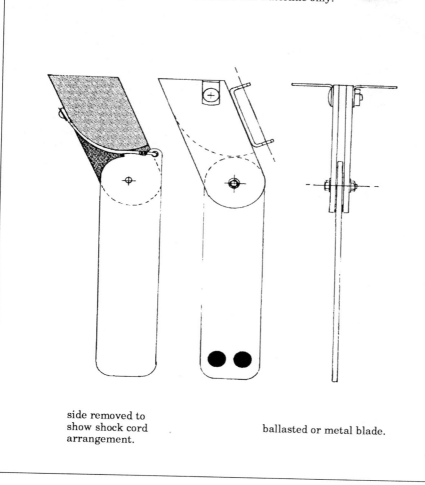

side removed to
show shock cord
arrangement.

ballasted or metal blade.

The rudder should be connected to the boat by a length of $1/4$ inch brass rod, brazing rod will do and can often be scrounged locally. It's also well worth the little extra bit of trouble to fit a retaining pin or a split rig at the bottom of the rudder pin to make sure that it can't come adrift while you're doing battle with the elements.

Of course boards and rudder should be finished off with primer, undercoat and two or three topcoats of a suitable colour paint, the ordinary household variety is quite good enough.

AN 'AUXILIARY' RUNNING SAIL

For sea canoeists in particular many miles of hard paddling can be saved with a simple running sail. It will not take the boat to windward but may be used whenever the wind is abaft the beam, it is a fair wind sail but none the less useful for that. The prime consideration in its design is that it should be simple and convenient to use.

As a running sail only its position on the boat is not critical and it can be stepped anywhere on the foredeck that is convenient. It could be stepped at the fore end of the cockpit but this will preclude the use of the spray deck while the sail is in use. A through deck mounting is best and the simplest arrangement although it does not require a lot of imagination to envisage a folding mast mounted in a tabernacle and hoisted by a running forestay. Such an arrangement would leave the canoe as near to normal when the sail was not in use as possible, and without the additional windage of the mast.

The mast and spar for this little wind engine are probably best made from aluminium tube, 1 inch diameter for the mast and $^3/_4$ inch dia. for the spar. The sail itself can be made up from 1 metre of 30 inch wide $1^1/_2$ oz spinnaker cloth. The added complication of the halyard has proved worthwhile in practice as it allows the sail to be set or doused at sea. Make sure that it is long enough to enable you to stow it under the deck lashings. The drawings of the rig are more or less self explanatory.

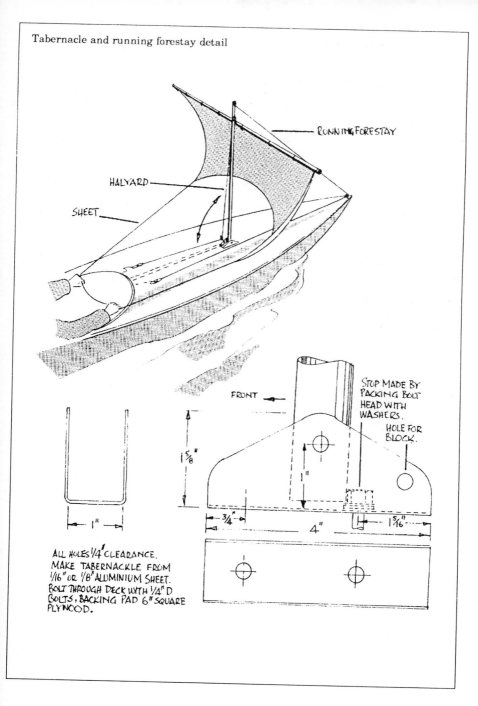

RUNNING FORESTAY

HALYARD

SHEET

FRONT

STOP MADE BY
PACKING BOLT
HEAD WITH
WASHERS.

HOLE FOR
BLOCK.

$1\frac{5}{8}"$

1"

$\frac{3}{4}"$

4"

$1\frac{5}{16}"$

ALL HOLES $\frac{1}{4}"$ CLEARANCE.
MAKE TABERNACKLE FROM
$\frac{1}{16}"$ OR $\frac{1}{8}"$ ALUMINIUM SHEET.
BOLT THROUGH DECK WITH $\frac{1}{4}"$ D
BOLTS, BACKING PAD 6" SQUARE
PLYWOOD.

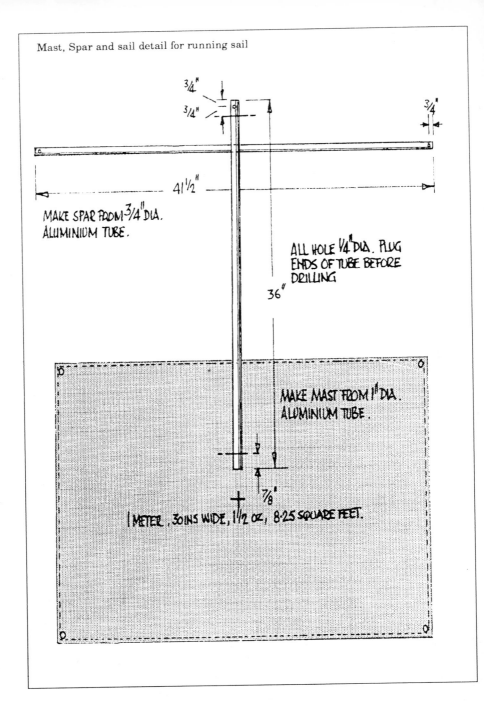

$\frac{3}{4}$"

$\frac{3}{4}$"

$\frac{3}{4}$"

41½"

MAKE SPAR FROM $\frac{3}{4}$" DIA. ALUMINIUM TUBE.

ALL HOLE ¼" DIA. PLUG ENDS OF TUBE BEFORE DRILLING

36"

MAKE MAST FROM 1" DIA. ALUMINIUM TUBE.

$\frac{7}{8}$"

1 METER, 30 INS WIDE, 1½ OZ, 8·25 SQUARE FEET.

The sailing canoe Little Pete. Designed and built by the writer, Little Pete is 13ft. O.A. and 28 ins beam, with a 30 sq. ft. Lateen sail. Plans and building instructions are available from Solway Dory, Angerton, Kirkbride, Carlisle CA5 5HX. Price £10.

SAILING YOUR CANOE

When all the business with nuts and bolts and pins and sailcloth is finished, the great day comes for your first sailing trials. Choose a quiet day if you can, not too much wind or you will become flustered and make mistakes. It will also help if there is not too big an audience, advice from the gallery is generally unhelpful and will only serve to confuse you.

Sailing, like so many other things, cannot really be learnt from a book. You just have to get out there and do it. The best education of all is experience and you must be prepared to serve your time.

For your first few trips all you really need to remember is that when the wind makes the boat heel too much for your peace of mind then all you have to do is to release the mainsheet, that is the rope that controls the boom. As soon as you let go of the mainsheet the press of the wind is spilt from the sail, the sail will weathercock into the wind and the boat will come upright again. It really is as simple as that. The one thing you must NEVER do is to tie the mainsheet off to a cleat or some such, it must always be in your hand ready for instant easing or release if the boat shows signs of being overpowered.

When you set off on your first trip, if its possible pick a day when the wind is blowing parallel to the shore. Paddle clear of the beach with the mainsheet slack and the sail weathercocking into the wind, until you have room about you to sail. Gently pull in the mainsheet, you will feel the press of the wind as soon as you do and the boat will start to move. If you're using a paddle to steer with this should be under your leeward arm, steer by rotating the paddle shaft about its own axis rather than by pivoting the paddle like a tiller. You will soon notice that without the board down the canoe will sail quite well once the wind is coming from over your shoulder and on this point of sailing it is usual to raise the board to reduce the drag. A leeboard would float to the surface under these conditions and can just be left to trail along beside the boat unless you are in a really 'go fast' situation when it can be brought inboard.

As you turn the boat up into the wind, so that you feel the wind on your face, you will find that without the board down she will keep sliding off downwind, to leeward. This is when you need the leeboard or daggerboard and it can do its job of reducing this leeward drift. You will also need to have the sail fairly well sheeted in, perhaps almost in line with the boat.

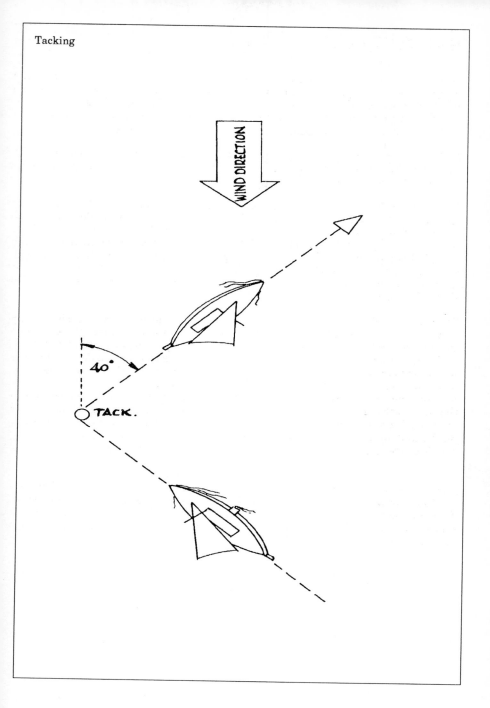

Don't try to sail directly into the wind, it's not on. The best you can expect is to be able to sail within forty degrees of the wind. A sailing boat makes progress into the wind by a series of tacks at an angle to the wind, first this way then that. A common mistake, even among experienced sailors, is to pinch the boat; that is to try to sail her pointing too much into the wind. The result is that the boat slows down as the angle to the wind is decreased. Much quicker progress will be made if you allow the boat to sail a little more off the wind and put in an extra tack or two.

Sailing into the wind or even across the wind with the sail more or less in line with the boat is what is called sailing close hauled. It is in this mode that you are most likely to face a capsize, particularly if there is a bit of a slop on the sea as well. Don't forget, especially if you have sailed in bigger boats, that what is no more than a merry dancing popple of a sea to the crew of a thirty footer can be, can turn out to be, trial by ordeal to a sixteen foot canoe. Get to know your boat and what she can take and always be ready to ease the mainsheet. At the risk of being boring it is worth saying again, you should always wear a lifejacket or buoyancy aid. I have sailed canoes at sea for many years and in that time have only once capsized and that was entirely my own fault. The point is that capsizes are rare if the boat is being handled in a seamanlike manner but when they come they take us completely by surprise. You will probably learn to sail your canoe with no difficulty at all and never the likelihood of getting your shirt wet, but that day will come.

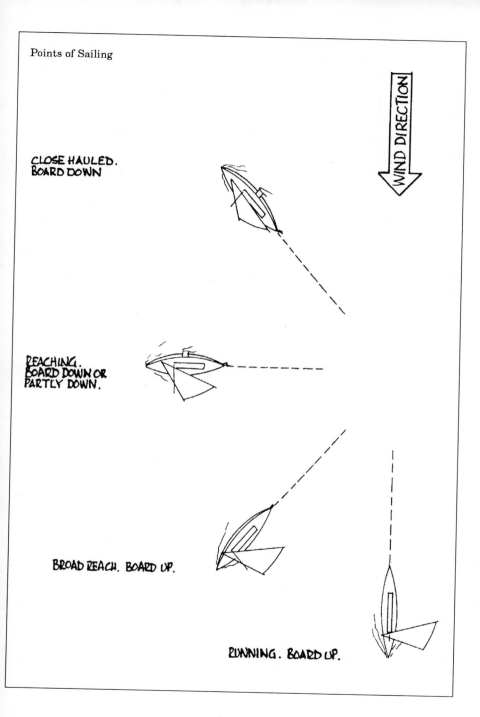

WIND DIRECTION

CLOSE HAULED.
BOARD DOWN

REACHING.
BOARD DOWN OR
PARTLY DOWN.

BROAD REACH. BOARD UP.

RUNNING. BOARD UP.

One other interesting point of sailing in a canoe is what is called gybing. This is the situation where the boat is running before the wind, you feel the wind over your shoulder, the sail is fairly well out perhaps almost at right angles to the boat. As you change course slightly, enough to bring the wind over the other shoulder the sail can be violently blown over onto the other side of the boat. This can be very dangerous and in the worst situation can cause a capsize. In a canoe gybing takes on a special significance because of their narrow beam, in bigger boats a violent gybe can bring the mast down. Under reasonable conditions however we do need to gybe in the course of normal navigation and so a tactic is employed. Watch the sail carefully once the rudder has been put over, as the sail swings over allow the sheet to run freely through your hand and only slowly increase your grip on the sheet. The sail should be allowed to swing right through, perhaps as much as one hundred and eighty degrees, you can always bring the sheet in a bit once the sail is on the new tack. Once you get used to doing this in light conditions you will find it all goes according to plan.

Gybing

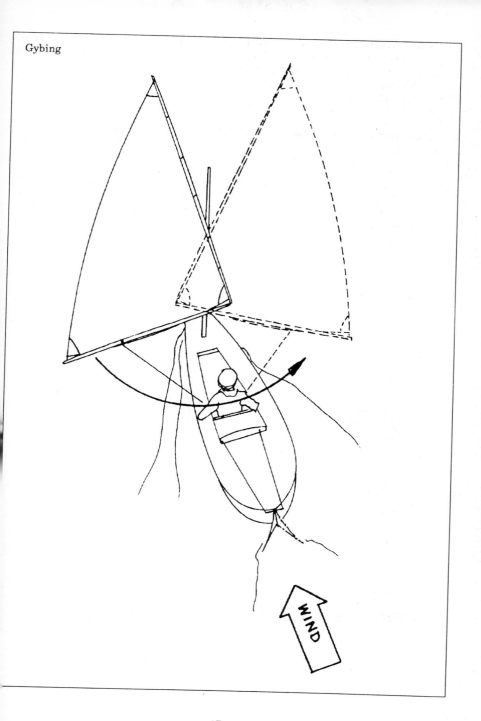

There are many sailing primers available at your local library that go into the theory of sailing in a great deal more depth and almost all that is applicable to sailing dinghies is true of sailing canoes, you just have to be a little more circumspect thats all. Learning to sail, like any other branch of canoeing takes time, but it is a very pleasurable time.

The Blandford-Bell 1960's sailing canoe. L.O.A. 15ft 6 ins, beam 2 ft. 4 ins. Construction, canvas skin on wooden frame. Weight, 56 lbs, sail area 40 sq. ft.

PADDLING YOUR CANOE
(For those who never have.)

The motto of the 'old boys' at the end of the last century was 'sail when you can and paddle when you must', and it is a formidable combination for the cruising boat. While it is not the intention of this work to give detailed instruction on paddling technique some basics may be useful to those readers who are perhaps coming to canoeing for the first time.

The most obvious difference between rowing and paddling is that the paddler is facing forwards in the direction he is travelling and of course there is not the mechanical advantage of a fulcrum available to the paddler. You can use either a double bladed kayak paddle or a single bladed paddle, as you prefer. If it is the former then get used to paddling with the blade feathered, that is set at right angles to one another, right from the start. Feathering reduces the wind resistance on the blade that is in the air and can be very noticeable in a blow.

Grip the paddle with the hands slightly more than a shoulder's width apart.

The paddle is held in the right hand, for strokes on the left it is rotated through ninety degrees by the right hand only.

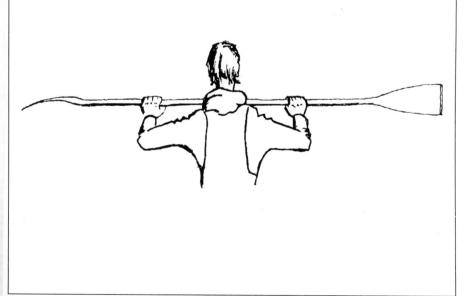

49

Grasp a double bladed paddle with your hands slightly more than a shoulders width apart, reach forward with a blade towards the bow of the boat so that it enters the water at about fortyfive degrees. Pull back steadily with the blade almost fully immersed and lift it from the water as it passes your hips. The opposite blade will now be well on its way towards entering the water and the process can be repeated ad nauseum.

For the cruising boat, which may have many hours of paddling in front of it, the most important part of the technique is that the paddle strokes are long and low and slow.

Turning in a sailing canoe is usually accomplished by using the rudder, even when paddling but it is sometimes useful to be able to turn the boat more quickly, perhaps at a dockside or in a restricted creek. This can be achieved by simply paddling forward on one side and backwards on the other, the canoe will then literally turn on a sixpence.

By paddling backwards, with the power being directed towards the bow, the canoe can be made to go backwards. You can use the rudder too while going astern and the boat will go in the direction that the rudder is pointing in, but this is such an unfamiliar mode to most of us that it is seldom used and perhaps hardly worth the trouble of learning.

The Slap Support stroke. Practise on both sides. Close your eyes and have a friend suddenly tip the canoe for you.

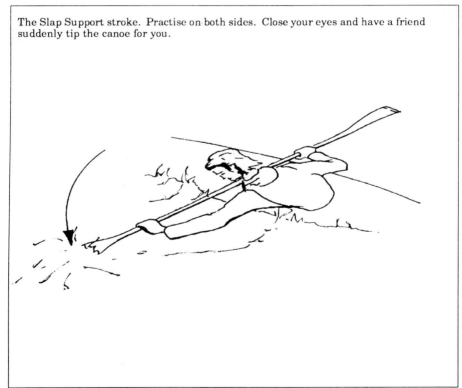

The other basic paddle stroke that can sometimes be useful to the canoe sailor is the slap support stroke. It is very quick and can be used to good effect in an emergency if you have your paddle in your hand at the time. As the canoe rolls in a threatening manner, reach out at right angles to the boat and in the same direction as the roll and slap the flat of the blade down hard onto the surface of the water. With a combination of pulling yourself towards the supporting paddle and strong hip movement the impending capsize can be averted quite easily.

All of the basic paddle strokes for the double kayak paddle can equally well be used with a single bladed paddle. The biggest single difficulty that people have with the single paddle is in simply going straight. The basic stroke for the single paddle is the J stroke. The blade enters the water at about forty-five degrees and a little way out from the side of the boat, in the first third of the stroke the paddle is held so that the INNER edge of the blade is slightly forward of the outer edge. In the middle the blade is at right angles to the boat and for the last third of the stroke the paddle is again twisted so the the OUTER edge of the paddle is forward of the inner edge and the stroke finished by the blade pushing away from the boat. It sounds much more complicated than it really is and once you have learnt to do it you forget how. Of course canoe sailors have the advantage of a rudder to use, you can either cheat or use it to correct errors in your paddle strokes while you are learning.

The single bladed J stroke. The paddle may be recovered either by lifting it from the water or by slicing it back through the water.

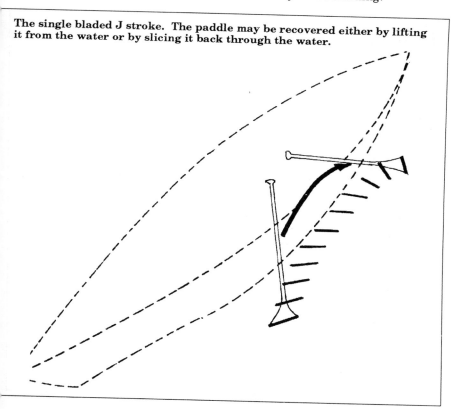

Whether or not you change sides while you're paddling is up to you, there is no great virtue in sticking doggedly to one side and the change does bring new muscles into use and rest others.

A much modified Klepper Aerius from the United States. This kind of multihull set up makes a fine coastal cruiser, capable of considerable distances. She is 17ft. O.A. and 35 ins. beam, her overall beam is 10 ft. The outriggers are made from polythene tubes filled with foam and are 10 ins. diameter and 52 ins. long. The sail is 24 sq. ft. set on a gaff and a sprit boom.

AND FINALLY

Before you set out on your epic voyage do remember that although your boat can now travel greater distances it is your responsibility to see that she and her crew are properly equipped for the sea. If I am preaching to the converted then I crave your indulgence but it does seem to me that far too many people rush into situations that they are not equipped to handle. There is no virtue in being persuaded to go to sea if in YOUR opinion the conditions are not good enough or your boat is not equipped for such a venture.

Nor does it seem good seamanship to hang onto the mainsheet until you capsize as seems to be the habit of many dinghy sailors. Seamanship is not only the art of being able to conduct your craft from one place to another with safety but also in knowing when it is time to turn back or seek shelter. It is not only your safety that is at stake but also the anxiety and distress you may bring to others, family and friends. The sea, to which we gain access in our little craft may be the last great adventure available to so many of us, we must treat it with the respect it deserves less the Whitehall mandarins take it from us as has happened in France.

Adventure by all means, that is what sailing canoes are for but ADVENTURE SAFELY.

If like me you live in the sticks then you may have problems in finding suppliers. I depend largely on mail order and a couple of very good firms are:

Thomas Foulkes,
8a Sansom Road,
Leytonstone,
London E11 3HB

and,

Jack Holt Ltd.,
The Embankment,
Putney,
London SW15 1LG

They both will send you a catalogue and are stockists of sailing boat materials and equipment.

Two other useful sources of materials and gear are:

Granta Kayel Boats Ltd.,
29 Great Whyte,
Huntington,
Cambs. PE17 1EZ

and,

Valley Canoe Products Ltd.,
Private Road 4,
Colwick,
Nottingham NG4 2JT

These are rather more specialised in canoes and canoe equipment. Both will send you catalogues if you ask.

You will find it also rather difficult to get any books on sailing canoes, there is in fact quite a lot published but it is mostly all long out of print and largely unobtainable even from sources like The British Library and the National Maritime Museum.

Books that are in print and should be available from your local library, although you will have to ask them to obtain them for you are:

A Manual of Yacht and Boatbuilding by Dixon Kemp and recently reprinted by Ashford Press.

Building Classic Small Craft by John Gardiner.

Canoes and Canoeing by Percy Blandford and published by Lutterworth Press.

Pleasure Boating in the Victorian Era by P.A.L. Vine and published by Phillimore.

The Canoe by Roberts and Shackleton published by MacMillan of Canada.

There are also a couple of booklets that are easily obtainable:

Sixty Years in Small Boats by Dr. R.C.Anderson and obtainable from the National Maritime Museum, Greenwich, London,

and

A Short History of Canoeing by Oliver Cock and Published by the British Canoe Union, Flexel House, High Street, Addleston, Weybridge, Surrey

The Classic of them all must be,

Canoe and Boatbuilding by W.P. Stevens which is still obtainable in a photostat version from Earl G. Doan, 3556 W. Blakely Avenue NE, Bainbridge Island, Washington 98110–2205, U.S.A. The snag is that the drawings that go with the book are published separately by Mystic Seaport Museum, Mystic, Connecticut 06355, U.S.A.

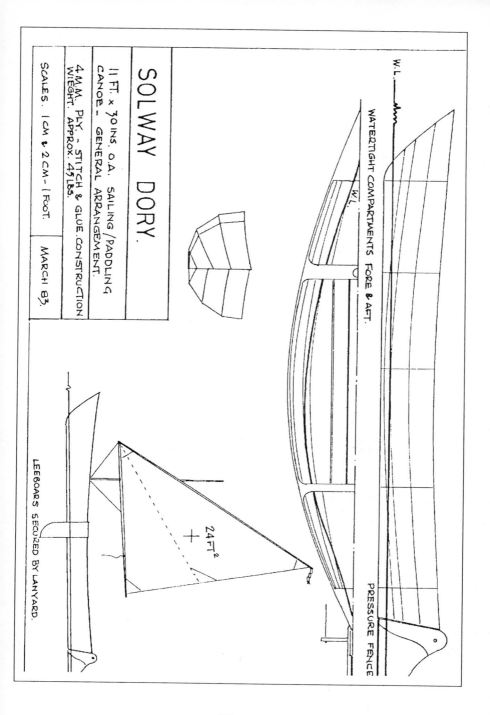

SOLWAY DORY.

11 FT. × 30 INS. O.A. SAILING / PADDLING CANOE. — GENERAL ARRANGEMENT.	
4 M.M. PLY. – STITCH & GLUE CONSTRUCTION. WIEGHT. APPROX. 45 LBS.	
SCALES. 1 CM = 2 CM = 1 FOOT.	MARCH 83.

W.L.

WATERTIGHT COMPARTMENTS FORE & AFT.

W.L.

PRESSURE FENCE

24 FT²

LEEBOARDS SECURED BY LANYARD.

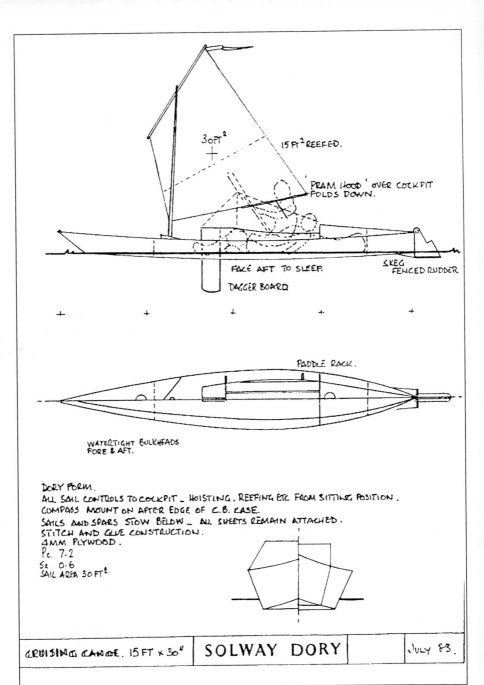

30ft^2

15ft^2 REEFED.

'PRAM HOOD' OVER COCKPIT FOLDS DOWN.

FACE AFT TO SLEEP.

DAGGER BOARD

SKEG
FENCED RUDDER

PADDLE RACK.

WATERTIGHT BULKHEADS
FORE & AFT.

DORY FORM.
ALL SAIL CONTROLS TO COCKPIT _ HOISTING. REEFING ETC FROM SITTING POSITION.
COMPASS MOUNT ON AFTER EDGE OF C.B. CASE.
SAILS AND SPARS STOW BELOW _ ALL SHEETS REMAIN ATTACHED.
STITCH AND GLUE CONSTRUCTION.
4MM PLYWOOD.
Pc. 7.2
St 0.6
SAIL AREA 30 FT^2.

CRUISING CANOE. 15 FT × 30"	SOLWAY DORY	JULY 83.

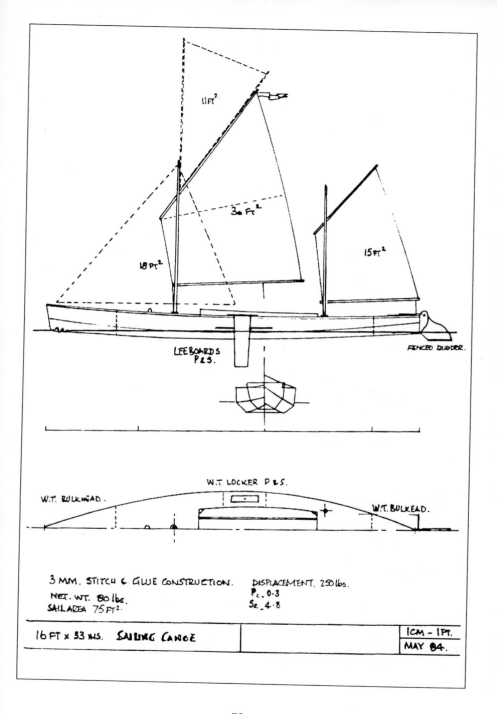

11 FT²

30 FT²

18 FT²

15 FT²

LEEBOARDS P&S.

FENCED RUDDER.

W.T. LOCKER P&S.

W.T. BULKHEAD.

W.T. BULKHEAD.

3 MM. STITCH & GLUE CONSTRUCTION.
NET. WT. 80 lbs.
SAIL AREA 75 FT².

DISPLACEMENT. 250 lbs.
P_c. 0.3
S_r 4.8

16 FT × 53 INS. SAILING CANOE		1CM – 1FT.
		MAY 84.

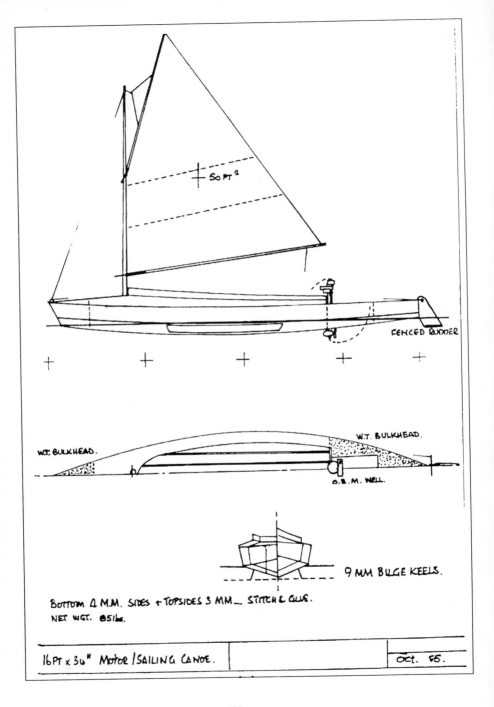

50 FT²

FENCED RUDDER

W.T. BULKHEAD.

W.T. BULKHEAD.

O.B.M. WELL.

9 MM BILGE KEELS.

BOTTOM 4 M.M. SIDES + TOPSIDES 3 MM — STITCH & GLUE.
NET WGT. 85 lbs.

16 FT x 36" MOTOR / SAILING CANOE.		OCT. 55.